the Complete FELINE HEALTH RECORD Book

Feline Health Record © 2021 Sosha Publishing

FELINE INFORMATION

NAME:

BIRTHDATE: | GENDER:

BREED: | SPAYED/NEUTERED:

COAT COLOR: | EYE COLOR:

MARKINGS: | DECLAWED:

OWNER(S):

ADDRESS:

PHONE: | CELL:

E-MAIL:

BREEDER/SHELTER:

DATE ACQUIRED: | REGISTERED NAME:

SIRE: | DAM:

TICA REGISTRY # | REGISTRATION TYPE:

CFA REGISTRY # | DNA #

MICROCHIP # | COMPANY:

VETERINARIAN:

EMERGENCY VET:

FELINE INFORMATION

WEIGHT	DATE	MEDICAL HISTORY
8 WEEKS:		
12 WEEKS:		
16 WEEKS:		
20 WEEKS:		
6 MONTHS:		
1 YEAR:		
2 YEARS:		
3 YEARS:		
4 YEARS:		
5 YEARS:		
6 YEARS:		
7 YEARS:		
8 YEARS:		
9 YEARS:		
10 YEARS:		
11 YEARS:		
12 YEARS:		
13 YEARS:		
14 YEARS:		

FELINE INFORMATION

WEIGHT	DATE	MEDICAL HISTORY
15 YEARS:		
16 YEARS:		
17 YEARS:		
18 YEARS:		
19 YEARS:		
20 YEARS:		

NOTES

VACCINATIONS

VACCINE	DATES					NOTE
FVRCP						
RABIES						
FeLV						
BORDETELLA						
FIV						
CHLAMYDIA FELIS						
FIP						

OTHER TREATMENTS

DEWORMING						
FLEA & TICK						

VACCINATIONS

VACCINE	DATES					NOTE
FVRCP						
RABIES						
FeLV						
BORDETELLA						
FIV						
CHLAMYDIA FELIS						
FIP						

OTHER TREATMENTS

DEWORMING						
FLEA & TICK						

VACCINATIONS

VACCINE	DATES					NOTE
FVRCP						
RABIES						
FeLV						
BORDETELLA						
FIV						
CHLAMYDIA FELIS						
FIP						

OTHER TREATMENTS

DEWORMING						
FLEA & TICK						

VACCINATIONS

VACCINE	DATES				NOTE
FVRCP					
RABIES					
FeLV					
BORDETELLA					
FIV					
CHLAMYDIA FELIS					
FIP					

OTHER TREATMENTS

DEWORMING					
FLEA & TICK					

VACCINATIONS

VACCINE	DATES					NOTE
FVRCP						
RABIES						
FeLV						
BORDETELLA						
FIV						
CHLAMYDIA FELIS						
FIP						

OTHER TREATMENTS

DEWORMING						
FLEA & TICK						

VET VISITATION LOG

DATE:	TIME:	VETERINARIAN:

REASON FOR VISIT:

TREATMENT PLAN:

MEDICATIONS:

VACCINATIONS:

VISIT NOTES

VET VISITATION LOG

DATE:	TIME:	VETERINARIAN:

REASON FOR VISIT:

TREATMENT PLAN:

MEDICATIONS:

VACCINATIONS:

VISIT NOTES

VET VISITATION LOG

DATE:	TIME:	VETERINARIAN:

REASON FOR VISIT:

TREATMENT PLAN:

MEDICATIONS:

VACCINATIONS:

VISIT NOTES

VET VISITATION LOG

DATE:	TIME:	VETERINARIAN:

REASON FOR VISIT:

TREATMENT PLAN:

MEDICATIONS:

VACCINATIONS:

VISIT NOTES

VET VISITATION LOG

DATE:	TIME:	VETERINARIAN:

REASON FOR VISIT:

TREATMENT PLAN:

MEDICATIONS:

VACCINATIONS:

VISIT NOTES

VET VISITATION LOG

DATE:	TIME:	VETERINARIAN:

REASON FOR VISIT:

TREATMENT PLAN:

MEDICATIONS:

VACCINATIONS:

VISIT NOTES

VET VISITATION LOG

DATE:	TIME:	VETERINARIAN:

REASON FOR VISIT:

TREATMENT PLAN:

MEDICATIONS:

VACCINATIONS:

VISIT NOTES

VET VISITATION LOG

DATE:	TIME:	VETERINARIAN:

REASON FOR VISIT:

TREATMENT PLAN:

MEDICATIONS:

VACCINATIONS:

VISIT NOTES

VET VISITATION LOG

DATE:	TIME:	VETERINARIAN:

REASON FOR VISIT:

TREATMENT PLAN:

MEDICATIONS:

VACCINATIONS:

VISIT NOTES

VET VISITATION LOG

DATE:	TIME:	VETERINARIAN:

REASON FOR VISIT:

TREATMENT PLAN:

MEDICATIONS:

VACCINATIONS:

VISIT NOTES

VET VISITATION LOG

DATE:	TIME:	VETERINARIAN:

REASON FOR VISIT:

TREATMENT PLAN:

MEDICATIONS:

VACCINATIONS:

VISIT NOTES

VET VISITATION LOG

DATE:	TIME:	VETERINARIAN:

REASON FOR VISIT:

TREATMENT PLAN:

MEDICATIONS:

VACCINATIONS:

VISIT NOTES

VET VISITATION LOG

DATE:	TIME:	VETERINARIAN:

REASON FOR VISIT:

TREATMENT PLAN:

MEDICATIONS:

VACCINATIONS:

VISIT NOTES

VET VISITATION LOG

DATE:	TIME:	VETERINARIAN:

REASON FOR VISIT:

TREATMENT PLAN:

MEDICATIONS:

VACCINATIONS:

VISIT NOTES

VET VISITATION LOG

DATE:	TIME:	VETERINARIAN:

REASON FOR VISIT:

_____

_____

_____

_____

TREATMENT PLAN:

_____

_____

_____

_____

MEDICATIONS:

VACCINATIONS:

_____

VISIT NOTES

_____

_____

_____

_____

_____

_____

VET VISITATION LOG

DATE:	TIME:	VETERINARIAN:

REASON FOR VISIT:

TREATMENT PLAN:

MEDICATIONS:

VACCINATIONS:

VISIT NOTES

VET VISITATION LOG

DATE:	TIME:	VETERINARIAN:

REASON FOR VISIT:

_____

_____

_____

_____

TREATMENT PLAN:

_____

_____

_____

_____

MEDICATIONS:

VACCINATIONS:

_____

VISIT NOTES

_____

_____

_____

_____

_____

VET VISITATION LOG

DATE:	TIME:	VETERINARIAN:

REASON FOR VISIT:

TREATMENT PLAN:

MEDICATIONS:

VACCINATIONS:

VISIT NOTES

VET VISITATION LOG

DATE:	TIME:	VETERINARIAN:

REASON FOR VISIT:

_____

_____

_____

_____

TREATMENT PLAN:

_____

_____

_____

_____

MEDICATIONS:

_____

VACCINATIONS:

_____

VISIT NOTES

_____

_____

_____

_____

_____

_____

VET VISITATION LOG

DATE:	TIME:	VETERINARIAN:

REASON FOR VISIT:

TREATMENT PLAN:

MEDICATIONS:

VACCINATIONS:

VISIT NOTES

VET VISITATION LOG

DATE:	TIME:	VETERINARIAN:

REASON FOR VISIT:

_____

_____

_____

_____

TREATMENT PLAN:

_____

_____

_____

_____

MEDICATIONS:

_____

VACCINATIONS:

_____

_____

VISIT NOTES

_____

_____

_____

_____

_____

_____

VET VISITATION LOG

DATE:	TIME:	VETERINARIAN:

REASON FOR VISIT:

_____

_____

_____

_____

_____

TREATMENT PLAN:

_____

_____

_____

_____

_____

MEDICATIONS:

_____

VACCINATIONS:

_____

_____

VISIT NOTES

_____

_____

_____

_____

_____

_____

VET VISITATION LOG

DATE:	TIME:	VETERINARIAN:

REASON FOR VISIT:

TREATMENT PLAN:

MEDICATIONS:

VACCINATIONS:

VISIT NOTES

VET VISITATION LOG

DATE:	TIME:	VETERINARIAN:

REASON FOR VISIT:

_____

_____

_____

_____

TREATMENT PLAN:

_____

_____

_____

_____

MEDICATIONS:

VACCINATIONS:

_____

VISIT NOTES

_____

_____

_____

_____

_____

_____

VET VISITATION LOG

DATE:	TIME:	VETERINARIAN:

REASON FOR VISIT:

TREATMENT PLAN:

MEDICATIONS:

VACCINATIONS:

VISIT NOTES

VET VISITATION LOG

DATE:	TIME:	VETERINARIAN:

REASON FOR VISIT:

_____

_____

_____

_____

TREATMENT PLAN:

_____

_____

_____

_____

MEDICATIONS:

_____

VACCINATIONS:

_____

_____

VISIT NOTES

_____

_____

_____

_____

_____

VET VISITATION LOG

DATE:	TIME:	VETERINARIAN:

REASON FOR VISIT:

_____

_____

_____

_____

TREATMENT PLAN:

_____

_____

_____

_____

MEDICATIONS:

VACCINATIONS:

_____

_____

VISIT NOTES

_____

_____

_____

_____

_____

VET VISITATION LOG

DATE:	TIME:	VETERINARIAN:

REASON FOR VISIT:

_____

_____

_____

_____

_____

TREATMENT PLAN:

_____

_____

_____

_____

_____

MEDICATIONS:

_____

VACCINATIONS:

_____

_____

VISIT NOTES

_____

_____

_____

_____

_____

_____

VET VISITATION LOG

DATE:	TIME:	VETERINARIAN:

REASON FOR VISIT:

_____

_____

_____

_____

TREATMENT PLAN:

_____

_____

_____

_____

MEDICATIONS:

VACCINATIONS:

_____

VISIT NOTES

_____

_____

_____

_____

_____

VET VISITATION LOG

DATE:	TIME:	VETERINARIAN:

REASON FOR VISIT:

_____

_____

_____

_____

TREATMENT PLAN:

_____

_____

_____

_____

MEDICATIONS:

_____

VACCINATIONS:

_____

VISIT NOTES

_____

_____

_____

_____

_____

VET VISITATION LOG

DATE:	TIME:	VETERINARIAN:

REASON FOR VISIT:

TREATMENT PLAN:

MEDICATIONS:

VACCINATIONS:

VISIT NOTES

VET VISITATION LOG

DATE:	TIME:	VETERINARIAN:

REASON FOR VISIT:

TREATMENT PLAN:

MEDICATIONS:

VACCINATIONS:

VISIT NOTES

VET VISITATION LOG

DATE:	TIME:	VETERINARIAN:

REASON FOR VISIT:

_____

_____

_____

_____

TREATMENT PLAN:

_____

_____

_____

_____

MEDICATIONS:

_____

VACCINATIONS:

_____

VISIT NOTES

_____

_____

_____

_____

_____

VET VISITATION LOG

DATE:	TIME:	VETERINARIAN:

REASON FOR VISIT:

TREATMENT PLAN:

MEDICATIONS:

VACCINATIONS:

VISIT NOTES

VET VISITATION LOG

DATE:	TIME:	VETERINARIAN:

REASON FOR VISIT:

TREATMENT PLAN:

MEDICATIONS:

VACCINATIONS:

VISIT NOTES

VET VISITATION LOG

DATE:	TIME:	VETERINARIAN:

REASON FOR VISIT:

TREATMENT PLAN:

MEDICATIONS:

VACCINATIONS:

VISIT NOTES

VET VISITATION LOG

DATE:	TIME:	VETERINARIAN:

REASON FOR VISIT:

TREATMENT PLAN:

MEDICATIONS:

VACCINATIONS:

VISIT NOTES

VET VISITATION LOG

DATE:	TIME:	VETERINARIAN:

REASON FOR VISIT:

_____

_____

_____

_____

_____

TREATMENT PLAN:

_____

_____

_____

_____

_____

MEDICATIONS:

VACCINATIONS:

_____

_____

VISIT NOTES

_____

_____

_____

_____

_____

VET VISITATION LOG

DATE:	TIME:	VETERINARIAN:

REASON FOR VISIT:

_____

_____

_____

_____

TREATMENT PLAN:

_____

_____

_____

_____

MEDICATIONS:

VACCINATIONS:

_____

VISIT NOTES

_____

_____

_____

_____

_____

VET VISITATION LOG

DATE:	TIME:	VETERINARIAN:

REASON FOR VISIT:

TREATMENT PLAN:

MEDICATIONS:

VACCINATIONS:

VISIT NOTES

FELINE
#2

FELINE

#2

FELINE INFORMATION

NAME:

BIRTHDATE: | GENDER:

BREED: | SPAYED/NEUTERED:

COAT COLOR: | EYE COLOR:

MARKINGS: | DECLAWED:

OWNER(S):

ADDRESS:

PHONE: | CELL:

E-MAIL:

BREEDER/SHELTER:

DATE ACQUIRED: | REGISTERED NAME:

SIRE: | DAM:

TICA REGISTRY # | REGISTRATION TYPE:

CFA REGISTRY # | DNA #

MICROCHIP # | COMPANY:

VETERINARIAN:

EMERGENCY VET:

FELINE INFORMATION

WEIGHT	DATE	MEDICAL HISTORY
8 WEEKS:		
12 WEEKS:		
16 WEEKS:		
20 WEEKS:		
6 MONTHS:		
1 YEAR:		
2 YEARS:		
3 YEARS:		
4 YEARS:		
5 YEARS:		
6 YEARS:		
7 YEARS:		
8 YEARS:		
9 YEARS:		
10 YEARS:		
11 YEARS:		
12 YEARS:		
13 YEARS:		
14 YEARS:		

FELINE INFORMATION

WEIGHT	DATE	MEDICAL HISTORY
15 YEARS:		
16 YEARS:		
17 YEARS:		
18 YEARS:		
19 YEARS:		
20 YEARS:		

NOTES

VACCINATIONS

VACCINE	DATES					NOTE
FVRCP						
RABIES						
FeLV						
BORDETELLA						
FIV						
CHLAMYDIA FELIS						
FIP						

OTHER TREATMENTS

DEWORMING					
FLEA & TICK					

VACCINATIONS

VACCINE	DATES					NOTE
FVRCP						
RABIES						
FeLV						
BORDETELLA						
FIV						
CHLAMYDIA FELIS						
FIP						

OTHER TREATMENTS

DEWORMING						
FLEA & TICK						

VACCINATIONS

VACCINE	DATES					NOTE
FVRCP						
RABIES						
FeLV						
BORDETELLA						
FIV						
CHLAMYDIA FELIS						
FIP						

OTHER TREATMENTS

DEWORMING						
FLEA & TICK						

VACCINATIONS

VACCINE	DATES				NOTE
FVRCP					
RABIES					
FeLV					
BORDETELLA					
FIV					
CHLAMYDIA FELIS					
FIP					
OTHER TREATMENTS					
DEWORMING					
FLEA & TICK					

VACCINATIONS

VACCINE	DATES					NOTE
FVRCP						
RABIES						
FeLV						
BORDETELLA						
FIV						
CHLAMYDIA FELIS						
FIP						

OTHER TREATMENTS

DEWORMING						
FLEA & TICK						

VET VISITATION LOG

DATE:	TIME:	VETERINARIAN:

REASON FOR VISIT:

_____

_____

_____

_____

TREATMENT PLAN:

_____

_____

_____

_____

MEDICATIONS:

VACCINATIONS:

_____

VISIT NOTES

_____

_____

_____

_____

_____

VET VISITATION LOG

DATE:	TIME:	VETERINARIAN:

REASON FOR VISIT:

TREATMENT PLAN:

MEDICATIONS:

VACCINATIONS:

VISIT NOTES

VET VISITATION LOG

DATE:	TIME:	VETERINARIAN:

REASON FOR VISIT:

TREATMENT PLAN:

MEDICATIONS:

VACCINATIONS:

VISIT NOTES

VET VISITATION LOG

DATE:	TIME:	VETERINARIAN:

REASON FOR VISIT:

_____

_____

_____

_____

_____

TREATMENT PLAN:

_____

_____

_____

_____

MEDICATIONS:

_____

VACCINATIONS:

_____

VISIT NOTES

_____

_____

_____

_____

_____

VET VISITATION LOG

DATE:	TIME:	VETERINARIAN:

REASON FOR VISIT:

TREATMENT PLAN:

MEDICATIONS:

VACCINATIONS:

VISIT NOTES

VET VISITATION LOG

DATE:	TIME:	VETERINARIAN:

REASON FOR VISIT:

TREATMENT PLAN:

MEDICATIONS:

VACCINATIONS:

VISIT NOTES

VET VISITATION LOG

DATE:	TIME:	VETERINARIAN:

REASON FOR VISIT:

_____

_____

_____

_____

TREATMENT PLAN:

_____

_____

_____

_____

MEDICATIONS:

VACCINATIONS:

_____

VISIT NOTES

_____

_____

_____

_____

_____

VET VISITATION LOG

DATE:	TIME:	VETERINARIAN:

REASON FOR VISIT:

TREATMENT PLAN:

MEDICATIONS:

VACCINATIONS:

VISIT NOTES

VET VISITATION LOG

DATE:	TIME:	VETERINARIAN:

REASON FOR VISIT:

_____

_____

_____

_____

TREATMENT PLAN:

_____

_____

_____

_____

MEDICATIONS:

VACCINATIONS:

_____

VISIT NOTES

_____

_____

_____

_____

_____

VET VISITATION LOG

DATE:	TIME:	VETERINARIAN:

REASON FOR VISIT:

TREATMENT PLAN:

MEDICATIONS:

VACCINATIONS:

VISIT NOTES

VET VISITATION LOG

DATE:	TIME:	VETERINARIAN:

REASON FOR VISIT:

TREATMENT PLAN:

MEDICATIONS:

VACCINATIONS:

VISIT NOTES

VET VISITATION LOG

DATE:	TIME:	VETERINARIAN:

REASON FOR VISIT:

TREATMENT PLAN:

MEDICATIONS:

VACCINATIONS:

VISIT NOTES

VET VISITATION LOG

DATE:	TIME:	VETERINARIAN:

REASON FOR VISIT:

_____

_____

_____

_____

TREATMENT PLAN:

_____

_____

_____

_____

MEDICATIONS:

VACCINATIONS:

_____

_____

VISIT NOTES

_____

_____

_____

_____

_____

VET VISITATION LOG

DATE:	TIME:	VETERINARIAN:

REASON FOR VISIT:

_____

_____

_____

_____

TREATMENT PLAN:

_____

_____

_____

_____

MEDICATIONS:

VACCINATIONS:

_____

VISIT NOTES

_____

_____

_____

_____

_____

VET VISITATION LOG

DATE:	TIME:	VETERINARIAN:

REASON FOR VISIT:

TREATMENT PLAN:

MEDICATIONS:

VACCINATIONS:

VISIT NOTES

VET VISITATION LOG

DATE:	TIME:	VETERINARIAN:

REASON FOR VISIT:

TREATMENT PLAN:

MEDICATIONS:

VACCINATIONS:

VISIT NOTES

VET VISITATION LOG

DATE:	TIME:	VETERINARIAN:

REASON FOR VISIT:

TREATMENT PLAN:

MEDICATIONS:

VACCINATIONS:

VISIT NOTES

VET VISITATION LOG

DATE:	TIME:	VETERINARIAN:

REASON FOR VISIT:

TREATMENT PLAN:

MEDICATIONS:

VACCINATIONS:

VISIT NOTES

VET VISITATION LOG

DATE:	TIME:	VETERINARIAN:

REASON FOR VISIT:

TREATMENT PLAN:

MEDICATIONS:

VACCINATIONS:

VISIT NOTES

VET VISITATION LOG

DATE:	TIME:	VETERINARIAN:

REASON FOR VISIT:

TREATMENT PLAN:

MEDICATIONS:

VACCINATIONS:

VISIT NOTES

VET VISITATION LOG

DATE:	TIME:	VETERINARIAN:

REASON FOR VISIT:

TREATMENT PLAN:

MEDICATIONS:

VACCINATIONS:

VISIT NOTES

VET VISITATION LOG

DATE:	TIME:	VETERINARIAN:

REASON FOR VISIT:

TREATMENT PLAN:

MEDICATIONS:

VACCINATIONS:

VISIT NOTES

VET VISITATION LOG

DATE:	TIME:	VETERINARIAN:

REASON FOR VISIT:

_____

_____

_____

_____

TREATMENT PLAN:

_____

_____

_____

_____

MEDICATIONS:

_____

VACCINATIONS:

_____

_____

VISIT NOTES

_____

_____

_____

_____

_____

_____

VET VISITATION LOG

DATE:	TIME:	VETERINARIAN:

REASON FOR VISIT:

TREATMENT PLAN:

MEDICATIONS:

VACCINATIONS:

VISIT NOTES

VET VISITATION LOG

DATE:	TIME:	VETERINARIAN:

REASON FOR VISIT:

_____

_____

_____

_____

TREATMENT PLAN:

_____

_____

_____

_____

MEDICATIONS:

_____

VACCINATIONS:

_____

_____

VISIT NOTES

_____

_____

_____

_____

_____

_____

VET VISITATION LOG

DATE:	TIME:	VETERINARIAN:

REASON FOR VISIT:

TREATMENT PLAN:

MEDICATIONS:

VACCINATIONS:

VISIT NOTES

VET VISITATION LOG

DATE:	TIME:	VETERINARIAN:

REASON FOR VISIT:

_____

_____

_____

_____

TREATMENT PLAN:

_____

_____

_____

_____

MEDICATIONS:

VACCINATIONS:

_____

VISIT NOTES

_____

_____

_____

_____

_____

VET VISITATION LOG

DATE:	TIME:	VETERINARIAN:

REASON FOR VISIT:

TREATMENT PLAN:

MEDICATIONS:

VACCINATIONS:

VISIT NOTES

VET VISITATION LOG

DATE:	TIME:	VETERINARIAN:

REASON FOR VISIT:

TREATMENT PLAN:

MEDICATIONS:

VACCINATIONS:

VISIT NOTES

VET VISITATION LOG

DATE:	TIME:	VETERINARIAN:

REASON FOR VISIT:

_____

_____

_____

_____

_____

TREATMENT PLAN:

_____

_____

_____

_____

_____

MEDICATIONS:

VACCINATIONS:

_____

_____

VISIT NOTES

_____

_____

_____

_____

_____

VET VISITATION LOG

DATE:	TIME:	VETERINARIAN:

REASON FOR VISIT:

_____

_____

_____

_____

TREATMENT PLAN:

_____

_____

_____

_____

MEDICATIONS:

VACCINATIONS:

_____

VISIT NOTES

_____

_____

_____

_____

_____

VET VISITATION LOG

DATE:	TIME:	VETERINARIAN:

REASON FOR VISIT:

TREATMENT PLAN:

MEDICATIONS:

VACCINATIONS:

VISIT NOTES

VET VISITATION LOG

DATE:	TIME:	VETERINARIAN:

REASON FOR VISIT:

TREATMENT PLAN:

MEDICATIONS:

VACCINATIONS:

VISIT NOTES

VET VISITATION LOG

DATE:	TIME:	VETERINARIAN:

REASON FOR VISIT:

TREATMENT PLAN:

MEDICATIONS:

VACCINATIONS:

VISIT NOTES

VET VISITATION LOG

DATE:	TIME:	VETERINARIAN:

REASON FOR VISIT:

TREATMENT PLAN:

MEDICATIONS:

VACCINATIONS:

VISIT NOTES

VET VISITATION LOG

DATE:	TIME:	VETERINARIAN:

REASON FOR VISIT:

_____

_____

_____

_____

TREATMENT PLAN:

_____

_____

_____

_____

MEDICATIONS:

_____

VACCINATIONS:

_____

VISIT NOTES

_____

_____

_____

_____

_____

VET VISITATION LOG

DATE:	TIME:	VETERINARIAN:

REASON FOR VISIT:

_____

_____

_____

_____

TREATMENT PLAN:

_____

_____

_____

_____

MEDICATIONS:

_____

VACCINATIONS:

_____

_____

VISIT NOTES

_____

_____

_____

_____

_____

_____

VET VISITATION LOG

DATE:	TIME:	VETERINARIAN:

REASON FOR VISIT:

_____

_____

_____

_____

_____

TREATMENT PLAN:

_____

_____

_____

_____

MEDICATIONS:

VACCINATIONS:

_____

VISIT NOTES

_____

_____

_____

_____

_____

_____

VET VISITATION LOG

DATE:	TIME:	VETERINARIAN:

REASON FOR VISIT:

TREATMENT PLAN:

MEDICATIONS:

VACCINATIONS:

VISIT NOTES

VET VISITATION LOG

DATE:	TIME:	VETERINARIAN:

REASON FOR VISIT:

_____

_____

_____

_____

_____

TREATMENT PLAN:

_____

_____

_____

_____

_____

MEDICATIONS:

VACCINATIONS:

_____

VISIT NOTES

_____

_____

_____

_____

_____

_____

Made in the USA
Las Vegas, NV
03 November 2024